Life in Numbers
Polls and Surveys

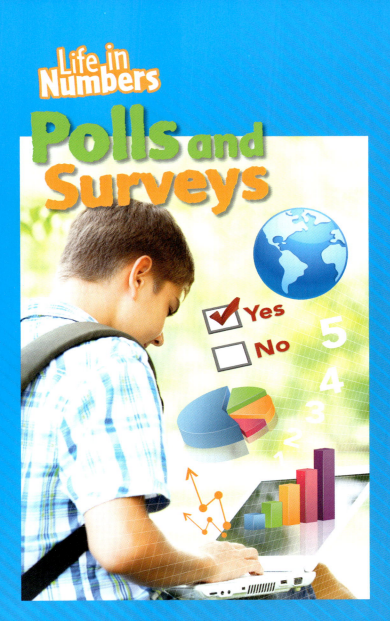

Monika Davies

Publishing Credits

Rachelle Cracchiolo, M.S.Ed., *Publisher*
Conni Medina, M.A.Ed., *Managing Editor*
Nika Fabienke, Ed.D., *Series Developer*
June Kikuchi, *Content Director*
John Leach, *Assistant Editor*
Regina Frank, *Graphic Designer*

TIME and the TIME logo are registered trademarks of TIME Inc. Used under license.

Image Credits: p.7 (left) Library of Congress [LC-DIG-pga-08442]; p.7 (center left) Library of Congress [LC-DIG-pga-00774]; p.7 (center right) Library of Congress [LC-DIG-pga-05346]; p.7 (right) Library of Congress [LC-USZ62-97178]; p.8 Library of Congress [LC-DIG-pga-07237]; p.9 National Archives [File no. SEN18A-J1]; p.12 Fine Art Images/Newscom; p.13 Everett Collection Historical/Alamy; p.15, p.37 (bottom) © TIME, Inc.; p.19 (right) Pictorial Press Ltd/Alamy; p.23 ClassicStock/Alamy; p.26 (insert) U.S. National Archives and Records Administration; p.26–27 National Archive/Newsmakers/Getty Images; p.29 Sipa via AP Images; p.29 (insert) Franklin D. Roosevelt Presidential Library; p.30 (top) Michael Vadon; p.30 (bottom) United States Department of State; p.32 AP Photo/John Minchillo; p.37 Splash News/Alamy; all other images from iStock and/or Shutterstock.

All companies and products mentioned in this book are registered trademarks of their respective owners or developers and are used in this book strictly for editorial purposes; no commercial claim to their use is made by the author or the publisher.

Library of Congress Cataloging-in-Publication Data

Names: Davies, Monika, author.
Title: Life in numbers : polls and surveys / Monika Davies.
Other titles: Polls and surveys
Description: Huntington Beach, CA : Teacher Created Materials, [2018] | Series: Life in numbers | Audience: Grades 7 to 8. | Includes bibliographical references and index.
Identifiers: LCCN 2017056442 (print) | LCCN 2018000389 (ebook) | ISBN 9781425854805 (e-book) | ISBN 9781425850050 (pbk. : alk. paper)
Subjects: LCSH: Public opinion polls--Juvenile literature. | Social surveys--Statistics--Juvenile literature. | Forecasting--Juvenile literature.
Classification: LCC HM1236 (ebook) | LCC HM1236 .D38 2018 (print) | DDC 303.3/8--dc23
LC record available at https://lccn.loc.gov/2017056442

Teacher Created Materials

5301 Oceanus Drive
Huntington Beach, CA 92649-1030
www.tcmpub.com

ISBN 978-1-4258-5005-0

© 2019 Teacher Created Materials, Inc.
Printed in China
Nordica.062018.CA21800492

Table of Contents

Polls vs. Surveys	4
A History of Asking and Tracking	6
Polls & Surveys: Step by Step	18
When Polls Get It Wrong	28
Polls in Daily Life	35
Shaping the Future	41
Glossary	42
Index	44
Check It Out!	46
Try It!	47
About the Author	48

Polls vs. Surveys

Do you think a survey is the same as a poll or the opposite of a poll?

This tricky question actually lacks a (completely) correct answer. While a survey is like a poll, each one has its own unique take on collecting data.

Surveys often pose a variety of questions for people to answer. Generally, they also include open-ended questions. These allow for unique and detailed responses that give more insightful feedback. In contrast, polls ask a limited number of questions with a **finite** set of answers. A poll's results offer a quick look at people's opinions on specific topics.

However, polls and surveys share a common goal: to collect data. And, in this age of the internet, knowledge is the most powerful tool at our disposal. Let's take a look at polls and surveys throughout history—and their impacts on our day-to-day lives.

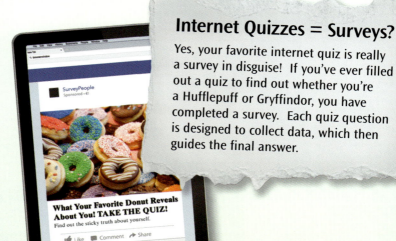

Internet Quizzes = Surveys?

Yes, your favorite internet quiz is really a survey in disguise! If you've ever filled out a quiz to find out whether you're a Hufflepuff or Gryffindor, you have completed a survey. Each quiz question is designed to collect data, which then guides the final answer.

Top 5 Sports of 1937 and 2013

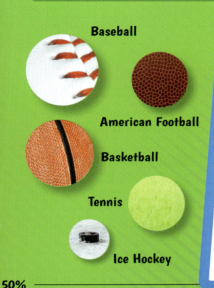

Baseball

American Football

Basketball

Tennis

Ice Hockey

✔ PEEK AT PAST POLLS

Throughout this book, we will peek at past **public opinion polls**. They range from silly to surprising to serious. Think about what kind of questions we find important to ask and what insight you can **glean** from each poll's findings. Watching sports is a popular U.S. pastime. See how the rankings have changed over the years.

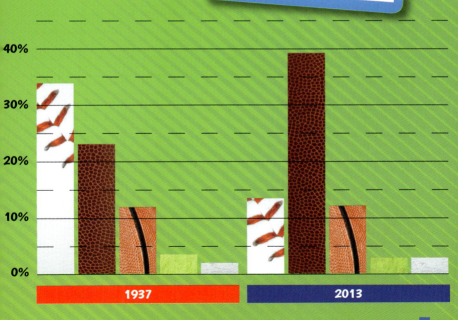

A History of Asking and Tracking

Humans are **inquisitive** creatures. We like to ask and answer questions. And we also enjoy seeing who agrees—and disagrees—with us. This has been true throughout history, especially when an election is on the line.

We often associate the word *poll* with election predictions. It makes sense then that the first official poll in American history was linked to a presidential election.

The First Political Poll

The year was 1824. As President James Monroe was retiring from politics, there was no clear favorite for the next president. The presidential race was shaping up to be tight. The two front-runners were clear: Andrew Jackson and John Quincy Adams. But who would take the lead?

A newspaper, the *Harrisburg Pennsylvanian*, came up with a straightforward solution to find out the likely victor. They simply asked voters which candidate they planned to vote for!

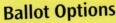

Ballot Options

What exactly did the ballot options look like for voters in 1824? The four choices for president were:

- Andrew Jackson, a senator from Tennessee
- John Quincy Adams, the secretary of state
- Henry Clay, the Speaker of the House
- William H. Crawford, the secretary of the treasury

THINK LINK

When there is an election on the horizon, newspapers devote sections to cover the predicted outcome. People put a lot of time into examining predictions. Consider the following questions:

> Why do people enjoy reading the predicted outcomes of events?

> Can reading about predicted outcomes affect future decisions? How?

> Do people put too much trust in the predictions they read about? Can too much trust be problematic?

In July 1824, the newspaper polled citizens in Wilmington, Delaware. The results were startling. Jackson had a seemingly commanding lead. Of the polled citizens, 70 percent picked him as their favorite. Adams was way behind with only 23 percent of the newspaper's tally. Clay and Crawford trailed even further with 4 percent and 2 percent. It seemed that an easy victory was in sight for Jackson.

But the newspaper's prediction was slightly off. In the election, Jackson did win the popular vote. But no candidate won the 131 **electoral votes** needed to have a majority at that time. Jackson won 99 votes, while Adams received 84.

According to the 12th Amendment, when no presidential candidate wins a clear majority, the House of Representatives has to choose the winner. In the end, the House chose Adams to become the next U.S. president.

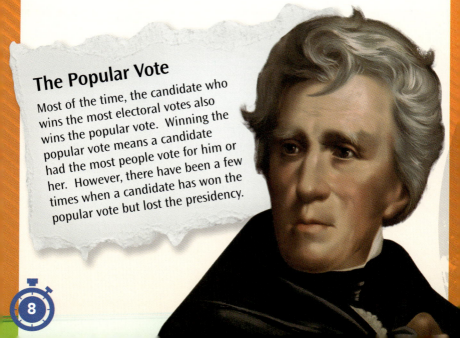

The Popular Vote

Most of the time, the candidate who wins the most electoral votes also wins the popular vote. Winning the popular vote means a candidate had the most people vote for him or her. However, there have been a few times when a candidate has won the popular vote but lost the presidency.

handwritten count of the votes in 1824

The Electoral College

Understanding the Electoral College is key to understanding American elections. Each state has an assigned number of electoral votes. When a presidential candidate wins a state, he or she wins that state's electoral votes. In 1824, a candidate needed 131 electoral votes. Today, the first candidate to win 270 electoral votes is the next president.

The results from the first political poll in the United States were technically wrong. Yet the poll had predicted the public's opinion correctly. Jackson had been the popular favorite in the newspaper's poll. And, in the election, he won the popular vote easily.

The public was intrigued with these results. Soon, other news outlets began using polls to predict elections. A polling trend had officially launched.

President Jackson...Finally

Even though Jackson lost in 1824, he ran for president again in 1828 and defeated Adams. He received 178 electoral votes, and Adams only received 83. Jackson served for eight years.

The Straw Poll

The newspaper's polling method had been simple. All it involved was asking a selection of people which presidential candidate was their favorite. The term **straw poll** was coined to describe this type of poll.

A straw poll is characterized by its informal nature. There is no science behind it. And straw polls can range from pinpoint accuracy to being widely off base. However, for over a century, straw polls were the go-to method to predict election results.

These early straw polls relied on a simple strategy—the more people polled, the more accurate the result would be. Straightforward, right? But that understanding shifted completely in 1936.

A Windy Outlook

Conducting a straw poll has been said to be just like "throwing straws in the wind." Farmers would throw handfuls of straw in the air to see which way the wind blew them. A straw poll did the same. It asked a question to see where people's opinions were. This is likely how the name originated!

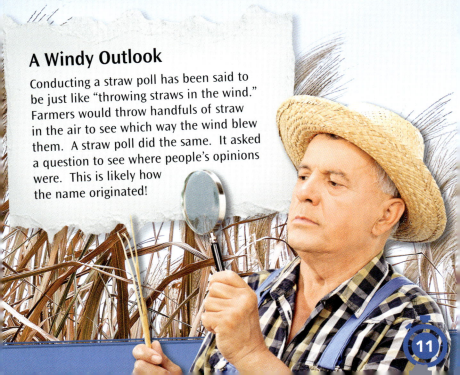

Soviet cosmonaut Yuri Gagarin was the first person to orbit Earth.

✔ PEEK AT PAST POLLS

Checking in on past polls can give us interesting historical insights. It can also provide a unique glimpse into the public's perspective at the time. In December 1959, the Gallup Poll asked Americans, "Which country—the United States or the Soviet Union—do you think will be first to send a man into outer space?" Here is how people responded. What do the numbers reveal about how Americans felt?

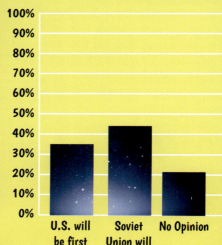

1959: Space Race

Literary Digest vs. Gallup

In the early twentieth century, *Literary Digest* ruled the magazine world. It had correctly predicted the results in four presidential elections. This earned the magazine a huge readership.

However, the 1936 election was a game changer for polls. Voters were choosing between Alf Landon and Franklin D. Roosevelt. *Literary Digest* sent out 10 million questionnaires to find out which candidate the public planned to vote for. Over two million responses were received.

The magazine tallied the replies. It boldly predicted that Landon would take 57 percent of the vote. Roosevelt would trail behind with only 43 percent.

But a new face in the polling world had a different perspective. Enter George Gallup.

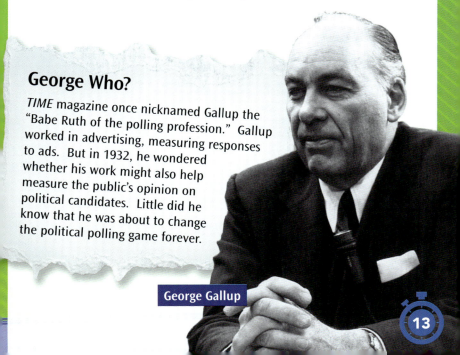

George Who?

TIME magazine once nicknamed Gallup the "Babe Ruth of the polling profession." Gallup worked in advertising, measuring responses to ads. But in 1932, he wondered whether his work might also help measure the public's opinion on political candidates. Little did he know that he was about to change the political polling game forever.

George Gallup

Gallup polled 50,000 people about the election. *Literary Digest* had polled 40 times more people. Yet Gallup also had a bold prediction. He stated that Roosevelt would be the nation's next leader. And he was right! Roosevelt ended up taking home 62 percent of the popular vote in his 1936 landslide victory.

What was the fatal flaw in *Literary Digest*'s polling method? Even though the response to its poll was large, it was not a **representative sample**. *Literary Digest* only polled a certain group of people. These people either had a 1936 auto registration or were listed in the phone book. But many Roosevelt supporters did not own a car or telephone. In contrast, Gallup polled a random selection. This **yielded** more accurate data.

Literary Digest was mocked for its error. The magazine went out of business. But this prediction elevated Gallup to new heights. His company was—and still is—heralded as one of the nation's most trusted polling organizations.

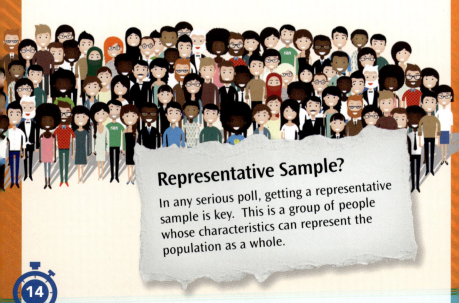

Representative Sample?
In any serious poll, getting a representative sample is key. This is a group of people whose characteristics can represent the population as a whole.

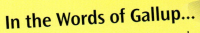

In the Words of Gallup...

Gallup once said, "Polling is merely an instrument for **gauging** public opinion. When a president, or any other leader, pays attention to poll results, he is, in effect, paying attention to the views of the people." Consider this as you read on, and decide whether you agree with Gallup's views.

Long-Term Gallup Polls

These days, the Gallup Poll focuses on conducting public opinion polls. These polls measure public opinion on a range of topics. These include political, social, and economic issues.

Some of these polls have been repeated many times over the decades. Here are the results from two of these long-term polls:

People were asked, **"If your party nominated a generally well-qualified person for president who happened to be black would you vote for that person?"** The graph below shows how people answered. What changed in the 1960s so that the majority of Americans said they would vote "yes"?

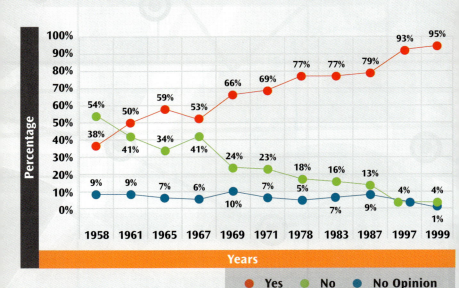

In another poll, people were asked, **"What do you think is the ideal number of children for a family to have?"** The responses are shown in the graph below. Why do you think the ideal number of children changed from 1967 to 1973?

● 0-2   ● 3+

Polls & Surveys: Step by Step

First, there was a century of straw polls with hit-or-miss results. Then, in 1936, Gallup brought in a more scientific approach to polling the public. Today, polling involves a very **systematic** approach. This approach has been tweaked over the decades. Let's examine the to-do list of a **pollster** in today's world.

First: Pick a Population

First, pollsters must identify the **target population** that their polls seek to represent. Some polls look at a specific group of people. But most public opinion polls aim to speak for the country's whole population. For American pollsters, this refers to everyone over 18 years old in the United States.

Transparency in Action

There are several things a pollster must tell you before asking any questions. This includes the total sample size and a definition of the population under study. They must also explain how people were selected. A reputable pollster will strive to be as **transparent** as possible about the survey.

1948: Women and Slacks

✔ PEEK AT PAST POLLS

At one time in history, it was not common for women to wear "slacks" (long pants). In January 1948, the Roper Center and Gallup Poll asked Americans, "Do you approve or disapprove of women of any age wearing slacks in public?" The results are listed to the right.

At Home	In Public
65% Approve	**32%** Approve
11% Disapprove	**44%** Disapprove
24% Indifferent/ Not sure	**26%** Indifferent/ Not sure

Aviator Amelia Earhart and actress Katharine Hepburn often wore slacks before they were fashionable.

19

Second: Take a Random Sample

Once a target population is in place, pollsters need to question a random sample of people. To do so, they must avoid falling into two traps.

First, the sample size cannot be too small. Typically, the more people polled, the more accurate the result will be. However, over time, pollsters have discovered a smaller sample size can still yield accurate results. As we saw with the *Literary Digest* fiasco, a larger sample does not always equal accurate data.

Second, the sample size cannot be too narrow. Pollsters must be careful that their polling sample is as **diverse** as possible. For starters, this means the sample must include a range of ages, genders, races, incomes, and regions.

The Perfect Sample Size

What do you think is the perfect sample size for a poll? Most polling organizations aim for the sweet spot of 1,000 to 1,500 respondents. Research has shown that increasing the number beyond that target range does not increase accuracy in any **substantial** way. Polling fewer people also brings a survey's overall cost down.

Soup-tacular!

When you're making soup, you don't need to taste the entire batch to know what it tastes like. If you have stirred the pot correctly, a taste test will tell you exactly how the soup has turned out. In a similar way, a random sample acts as a "taste test" of the population's overall opinion on an issue.

Third: Choose a Method

Polling methods have changed over the years. At one point, pollsters went door-to-door to conduct their surveys. By about 1986, most American households had phones. So calling people to ask them questions quickly became the best polling method.

Nowadays, many leading polling organizations still rely mainly on phone interviews. But now, a variety of polling methods, such as internet surveys, are also employed.

Fourth: Don't Show Bias

Polling questions must be worded carefully. Depending on how a question is phrased, people might unconsciously react to hidden **bias** in the wording. For instance, one Gallup Poll examined the support for a U.S. military presence in Bosnia. There were two ways to frame the poll's question. Pollsters could say the United States was "sending troops." Or they could say the United States was "contributing troops." This one-word change could completely alter a person's response.

Declining the Call

The Pew Research Center is a well-known polling organization. In 1997, its response rate for telephone calls was 36 percent. In 2017, that response rate dropped to 9 percent. In 1997, a polling organization looking for a sample of 800 respondents had to make 2,000 to 2,500 calls. Just 20 years later, 7,500 to 9,000 calls were required to get that same sample size.

polling in the 1970s

Pushy Polls

A reputable pollster will not attempt to sway a respondent's answer in any way. However, during election seasons, push polls are a tactic sometimes used to mislead respondents. These are not genuine polls; instead, push polls ask leading questions that prompt or encourage people to answer a certain way.

Fifth: Weight the Sample

Pollsters have no way of knowing who will reply to their surveys. Of course, they work hard to obtain a random sample of replies. But that's only one part of the equation for a representative sample. Pollsters also must match the sample's **demographics** to the overall population. This calls for a balancing strategy known as *weighting*.

Every poll receives a variety of replies. They come from people of different age brackets, regions, genders, races, and incomes. Each reply is assigned a "weight." Once all the data is collected, pollsters look at the demographics of their sample. Then, they compare it with the overall population's demographics. They may find one demographic is underrepresented. Replies from that bracket are then weighted higher. Another demographic could be overrepresented. Those replies are weighted lower.

Weighting a sample is a very fine balancing act. The strategy is based in science, but it's not a foolproof practice.

Language Barriers

To save money and avoid translation complications, most polls are done in English. However, what about households where English is not the first language? According to the Pew Research Center, 73 percent of Latinos speak Spanish at home. So, an English-speaking pollster's sample of the Latino population is likely to not be representative of the whole.

Spooky Survey

✔ **PEEK AT PAST POLLS**

Through the years, the Gallup Poll has asked Americans some unique questions. On Halloween in 2000, people were asked, "Do you believe in ghosts?" About 30 percent of Americans said yes. In 1978, when asked the same question, only 11 percent of American adults said they believed in ghostly haunts. It seems our belief in the paranormal has spiked in the last few decades!

Approval Rating

Since 1945, which U.S. president has had the highest overall average approval rating? John F. Kennedy had an overall 70.1 percent approval rating during his short time in office. In contrast, Richard Nixon had an overall approval rating of 49 percent and a low point of 24 percent approval in 1974.

President John F. Kennedy

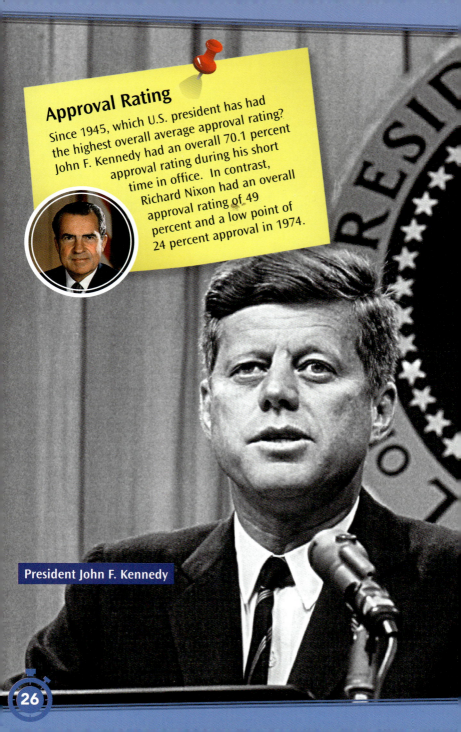

Sixth: Interpret the Results

And the results are in. It's time to analyze the findings! For pollsters, **context** is the key ingredient to understanding their data. Comparing the findings to past data allows for a deeper understanding of the issue at hand. This is vital to a critical examination of polling results.

For example, consider the following question: Do you approve or disapprove of the way (the president) is handling his job as president?

Since 1945, this question has been asked of the American public. The responses **relay** the current president's "job approval rating." This rating is tallied throughout the year. Pollsters regularly track the ups and downs of this number. They also compare this rating to those of previous presidents.

Looking at this rating offers insight into the public's perspective of the government. Context is what tells the poll's overall story.

Your Turn!

Remember, when you read the results of a public opinion poll, you also must look at the findings with a critical eye. Are there any chances for bias in the poll? Did the pollsters employ best practices? As a media consumer, this is your job!

When Polls Get It Wrong

Since 1936, polls and surveys that track public opinion have become quite scientific. But that doesn't mean they are **infallible**. The following case study is a reminder that even with twenty-first century science, polling predictions can often miss the mark.

2016 Election: Clinton vs. Trump

On November 8, 2016, Americans voted for their next president. Two names topped the ballot: Hillary Clinton and Donald Trump.

That same day, pollsters posted their final predictions. The *New York Times* gave Clinton an 84 percent chance of victory. ABC News figured Clinton had 274 electoral votes for certain. Nearly every pollster predicted a surefire victory for Clinton. And they were all wrong.

Why November?

American presidential elections are always held in November on the first Tuesday after the first Monday. The reasoning for this timeline has its roots in the nineteenth century. Back then, America was an **agrarian** society. November marked the end of the fall harvest, and after spending their Sunday at church, farmers needed a full day of travel to get to voting stations on Tuesday.

one of the 2016 presidential debates

How to "Poll" Ahead

Today, many presidential candidates rely on public opinion polls to help shape their political strategies. In fact, some polls are privately **commissioned** by the candidates! This was not always common. The first president to use a private polling service was Franklin D. Roosevelt. His survey findings greatly influenced his public policies, as well as his campaign strategy.

On November 9, 2016, the tally was official. Trump had won 306 electoral votes. Clinton had 232 electoral votes. Pollsters were stunned. How did they all get it wrong? In the days that followed, pollsters debated their **botched** predictions. While there were likely many factors that led to this polling failure, three main theories emerged.

The Nonresponse Bias

The **nonresponse bias** has always been a **conundrum** for pollsters. This is a bias that happens when polling participants differ in significant ways from nonparticipants. For example, people who usually don't vote are unlikely to respond to a poll about which candidate they plan to vote for. Yet if that same group of people actually votes on Election Day, their votes are unaccounted for in the polls.

Some believe this is what happened with Trump's victory. People who were unlikely to respond to a poll voted for Trump in the election.

WRONG PREDICTIONS
Major media polls predicted the electoral votes each candidate would receive in the 2016 presidential election.

Polls	Clinton	Trump
Associated Press	274	190
Nate Silver and *FiveThirtyEight*	301	235
Princeton Election Consortium	304	215
Moody's Analytics	332	206
Los Angeles Times	352	186

Ways to Spend the Evening

✔ PEEK AT PAST POLLS

Gallup asked adults in the United States a simple question in three different years: "What is your favorite way to spend an evening?" Have a look at a few of the findings. Do any of the percentages surprise you? What do you think accounts for the changes in how adults spend their time?

	1986	2005	2015
Staying at home	13%	32%	34%
Television	34%	22%	16%
Resting/Relaxing	14%	8%	13%
Reading	14%	11%	12%
Going out	21%	10%	6%
Visiting with friends	8%	4%	6%

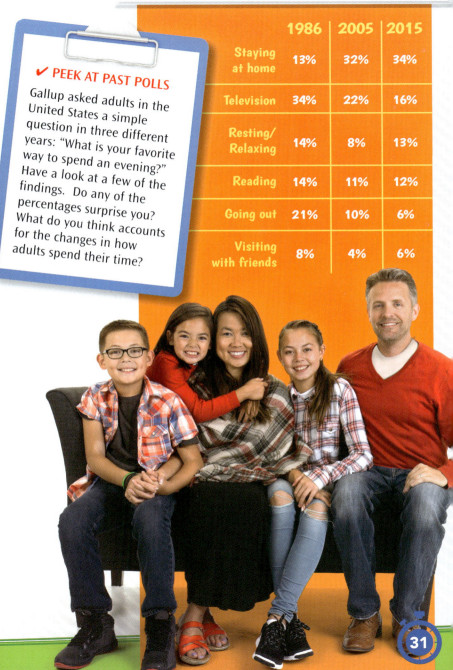

Socially Desirable Responses

The theory of the "Shy Trumper" stems from the idea of interviewer bias. People generally try to avoid disagreeing with each other. This is thought to influence the answers given to pollsters—especially during a phone interview. In other words, some people may tend to give answers they think pollsters want to hear.

"Shy Trumpers"

Some argued that it was the "Shy Trumpers" who tipped the polling scales. This is a nickname for Trump voters who didn't say they were voting for Trump when polled. But this theory applies only to polls over the phone, because people are more likely to answer truthfully online. Experts pointed out that online survey results weren't very different from the phone polls. While this was a common theory, it likely only accounted for a tiny percentage of polling error.

The "Likely Voter" Error

When people pick up the phone to talk to a pollster, most will say they intend to vote. However, some of those people will never make it to voting booths on Election Day.

Therefore, pollsters need to identify who is a likely voter. The results only include the replies of these likely voters. However, identifying likely voters is an inexact science. Some speculate this may have been a key failing in 2016's polling predictions.

Voter Turnout

In the 2016 presidential election, only 55.7 percent of the people in the United States who were able to vote did so. In terms of people voting, the United States lags far behind other developed nations. For example, in Australia, 79 percent of all eligible citizens voted that same year.

STOP! THINK...

It's no secret that Americans love their digital devices. But which digital devices do people use the most? In 2016, Nielsen, a polling company that examines **consumer trends**, gathered data on the percentage of time different age groups spent on different digital devices.

Percentage of Device Usage by Age

	18–34	35–49	50+
TV	31%	38%	56%
Radio	18%	18%	18%
TV Devices	11%	6%	3%
PC	10%	11%	8%
Smartphone	24%	20%	11%
Tablet	6%	7%	4%

> What are the biggest differences between the time spent on devices in the 18–34 group and the 50+ group?
> Do any of these numbers surprise you? Which ones, and why?
> If Nielsen polled people under the age of 18, what do you think the answers would be?

Polls in Daily Life

Polls and surveys can feel miles away from your day-to-day life, yet they've become an integral part of our existence, almost without us realizing it. Here are a few of the ways that polls and surveys factor into your life and make a difference.

What's for Dinner?

When it's time for dinner and no one can decide between pepperoni pizza and fried chicken, how does your family choose what to eat? If there are more than two people involved, you likely "poll" all hungry stomachs. Everyone is asked what they'd prefer—pizza or chicken—and the results are then tallied up. That's polling in action!

The Right Job

When you consider future job options, you might come across career quizzes online. These quizzes are filled with personality questions. As mentioned before, these quizzes are simply surveys in disguise! Each answer you give affects the results, which is exactly how a public opinion poll works.

Who's My Favorite Singer?

Most people have watched an episode of *American Idol* or *The Voice*. These shows encourage viewers to vote for their favorite singers. Dramatically, votes can make the difference between singers reaching their starry aspirations or wallowing in dashed dreams. Again, you are watching polling at work! Viewers have a finite number of choices. And the responses affect the final decision: who will stay and who will go?

2017: Spelling Matters

More likely to trust
2%

Less likely to trust
74%

Makes no difference
24%

✔ RECENT POLLING

In March 2017, an online poll asked, "If you saw a spelling or grammatical error in a politician's social media post, would it make you more likely or less likely to trust that they are doing a good job leading the country?" As you can see, most people lose confidence when politicians make errors in their posts.

American Idol judges and host

Top Influencers

One well-known poll is *TIME* magazine's annual "100 Most Influential People" list. Every year, different people end up on the list of pioneers, artists, leaders, titans, and icons who influence the world. The winner of the reader's poll is chosen by the public, but the rest are chosen by the staff at *TIME*.

Tough Choices

"Would you rather" questions present a fun way to peek into another person's **psyche**. Sometimes the results can be quite surprising! Here are four "would you rather" questions that people on the internet have answered. Does knowing how other people responded to each question make you reevaluate your own answer? What does each poll tell you about human personality?

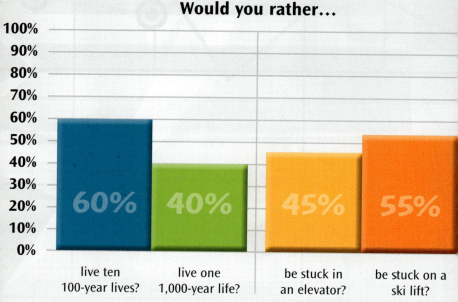

Would you rather...

- 60% live ten 100-year lives?
- 40% live one 1,000-year life?
- 45% be stuck in an elevator?
- 55% be stuck on a ski lift?

Source: funpolls.com

Would you rather…

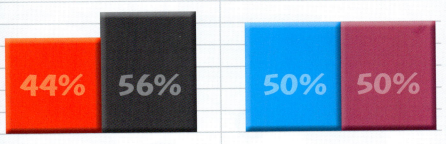

be a millionaire in the 1920s? | have $50,000 in 2015? | go to the past? | go to the future?

Shaping the Future

Polling is a complicated business. It's a practice that is in a constant state of improvement. Yet we still love to pore over public opinion results, comparing our answers with the final tallies. There's simply no escape from polls and surveys. They have swiftly become a part of our everyday existence.

When we answer a poll or a survey, we spend time in self-reflection. We ask ourselves, "What are my views on this topic?" And when we read the results of a poll or survey, we also reflect on those findings. Do the results match our own opinions? Or do these findings change the way we view particular issues?

Polls and surveys can define and redefine our perspective on a number of topics. As long as we question and examine their **methodologies** and results, polls and surveys have the power to guide the decisions that shape our future.

Winning Smiles

Here's one last poll result! On March 20, 2016, the Gallup Poll wanted everyone to know that, the day before, 72 percent of people in the world said they smiled.

Glossary

agrarian—of or relating to farms and farming

bias—a particular slant or attempted influence

botched—did (something) badly

commissioned—requested something be done

consumer trends—the general needs and wants of customers

context—the situation in which something happens

conundrum—a confusing or difficult problem

demographics—the qualities, such as age, sex, and income, of a specific group of people

diverse—made up of people or things that are different from one another

electoral votes—votes cast for president by representatives who are chosen by political parties in each state

finite—having a limit

gauging—making a judgment about measuring something

glean—to gather data little by little

infallible—not capable of being wrong or making mistakes

inquisitive—tending to ask questions; having a desire to know or learn more

methodologies—sets of rules used in processes

nonresponse bias—the bias that results when respondents differ in meaningful ways from nonrespondents

pollster—someone who makes questions for a poll, asks questions in a poll, or collects and presents results from a poll

psyche—the soul, mind, or personality of a person or group

public opinion polls—surveys designed to measure the public's views regarding a particular topic or series of topics

relay—to pass information along

representative sample—a small quantity of something, whose characteristics represent the entire batch, lot, or population

straw poll—an informal and unofficial poll or vote that is done to get information about what people think about something

substantial—important

systematic—using a careful system or method

target population—the entire group of people from which a sample might be drawn

transparent—honest and open; not secretive

yielded—produced information based on work or effort

Index

12th Amendment, 8

2016 U.S. Election. 28

ABC News, 28

Adams, John Quincy, 6, 8

Associated Press, 30

Bosnia, 22

Clay, Henry, 6, 8

Clinton, Hillary, 28, 30

Crawford, William, 6, 8

demographics, 24

election, 6–11, 13–14, 23, 28, 30, 33

Electoral College, 9

Gagarin, Yuri, 12

Gallup, George, 13–15, 18

Gallup Poll, 12, 16, 19, 22, 25, 41

government, 27

Harrisburg Pennsylvanian, 6, 10

House of Representatives, 6, 8

Jackson, Andrew, 6, 8, 10

job approval rating, 27

Kennedy, John. F., 26

Landon, Alf, 13

"likely voter" error, 33

Literary Digest, 13–14, 20

Los Angeles Times, 30

Monroe, James, 6

New York Times, 28

Nielsen, 34

Nixon, Richard, 26

Pew Research Center, 22, 24

pollster, 18, 20, 22–24, 27–28, 30, 32–33

popular vote, 8, 10, 14

public opinion polls, 5, 16, 18, 26–27, 36

push polls, 23

representative sample, 14, 24

Roosevelt, Franklin D., 13–14, 29

Roper Center, 19

sample size, 18, 20, 22

"Shy Trumper," 32–33

social media, 36

space race, 12

straw poll, 10–11, 18

TIME, 13, 37

Trump, Donald, 28, 30, 32–33

United States, 10, 12, 18, 22, 31, 33

Wilmington, DE, 8

Check It Out!

Websites

FiveThirtyEight. "FiveThirtyEight's Pollster Ratings." projects.fivethirtyeight.com/pollster-ratings/.

Smithsonian Magazine. "Inside the Alluring Power of Public Opinion Polls From Elections Past." www.smithsonianmag.com.

Pew Research Center. "Question Search." www.people-press.org/question-search/.

The Gallup Poll. "Timeline of Polling Events That Shaped the United States, and the World." www.gallup.com.

TIME. "How One Man Used Opinion Polling to Change American Politics." www.time.com/4568359/george-gallup-polling-history/.

TIME. "The 100 Most Influential People: 2017 List." www.time.com.

Videos

CrashCourse. "Public Opinion: Crash Course Government and Politics #33." www.youtube.com.

Pew Research Center. "Methods 101: Random Sampling." www.youtube.com.

Try It!

A big debate has started at your school: should cell phones be incorporated into classroom lessons? Your teachers want to know how you and your fellow students feel about this. Your assignment is to poll a representative sample of the student population and present your findings.

- ✔ How many students should you survey for accurate results? How can you ensure you target a representative sample?

- ✔ How should you poll your fellow classmates? What will be your most effective strategy?

- ✔ Craft your poll or survey questions, making sure they do not have bias.

- ✔ Share your plan and poll questions with some classmates. Do they agree with your methodology? Do they think your questions are unbiased?

About the Author

Monika Davies is a Canadian writer and traveler. She loves answering career quizzes, although strangely, they all conclude she should have been a funeral director. There is also an 87.2 percent chance she's taken a Hogwarts sorting quiz. (She is definitely a Hufflepuff!)

Davies graduated from the University of British Columbia with a bachelor of fine arts in creative writing. She has written over 20 books for young readers.